To

From

Date

Barbara Rainey

When *Christmas* Came

FAMILYLIFE PUBLISHING®

WHEN CHRISTMAS CAME
Published by FamilyLife Publishing®
5800 Ranch Drive
Little Rock, Arkansas 72223
1-800-FL-TODAY • FamilyLife.com
A ministry of Campus Crusade for Christ, Inc.

Scripture quotations are from The Holy Bible, English Standard Version, copyright ©2001 by Crossway Bibles, a division of Good News Publishers. Used by permission. All rights reserved.

ISBN: 978-1-60200-248-7

FamilyLife Publishing® is a registered trademark of FamilyLife, a ministry of Campus Crusade for Christ, Inc.

Design: The DesignWorks Group, www.thedesignworksgroup.com
Author photo: J.E. Stover Photography, Inc.

Printed in the United States of America
2008—First Edition

12 11 10 09 08   1 2 3 4 5

This book is dedicated to

Molly Ann Mutz

my namesake,

my precious granddaughter,

who because Christmas came

we will see again one day,

when all things

will be made new!

June 13-19, 2008

Christmas
is all about God.

Christmas is all about God.

It was His stunning idea
in the beginning
before time began.
No one has seen the Father,
the all-seeing One,
the Three in One,
the Almighty,
the Alpha and the Omega,
Who sees and hears and knows all,
yet loves His children.
With God nothing is impossible.
A virgin birth?
God of the universe in infant form?
A perfect life?
Nothing is too difficult for God.

Christmas

For God so

is about Love.

loved ...

For God so loved ...

Christmas
is about Love.
For God is Love,
unchanging, everlasting,
abounding, steadfast love
that never ceases.
Love beyond comprehension,
enduring forever.
He set His heart in love
on me.
Great in love.
Rich in kindness.
Rich in patience
toward us.
Love never fails.

There was much more to discover about this babe in the manger and the love that had sent Him.

Christmas Is About Love

As a child, I delighted in every aspect of the holiday season—the music, the decorations, the gift-giving, and even the weather. Through my eyes, everything in our small Midwest town was touched by Christmas wonder, from the tidy homes with manger scenes on the lawns to schools, churches, and businesses displaying colorful lights and candles in their frosted windows. It was all magical.

With the first cold spell every October, I began to anticipate the transformation of the Christmas season to come. I couldn't wait for it to arrive and I always wanted it to last forever.

As I grew up, my mother allowed me to take over more of the decorating and preparations at home. Perhaps she secretly enjoyed my eagerness, and the freedom it gave her to do other things. My festive creations spread from our simple tree and manger scene to boughs of greenery in the front hall and on the fireplace mantel, candles and Santas and ribbons on tabletops, a special floral arrangement on the dining room table, and of course, plates of our favorite cookies all cut in the shapes of snowmen, Santa Claus, angels, and stars, and sprinkled with red and green sugars. In my eyes, nothing our family did the rest of the year compared to our preparations for Christmas.

Looking back, I see that the wonderment of my childhood Christmases, and the longing I felt to keep it with me forever, was an invitation God was writing on my heart. He wanted me to experience something far greater than my present-tense life. There was so much more to discover about this babe in the manger and the love that had sent Him. Christmas really could last forever.

God was calling me every year at Christmas.

He still speaks and invites us to Himself. Such is the nature of God's love. He is ever pursuing, and always ready to receive us.

Christmas is about love, because God is love.

For God so loved ...

For the

Christmas

is about the

God so loved World...

World.

For God so loved

the world...

Christmas
is about the World.
All
6,600,224,175
of us
in this world.
Created in His image,
a little lower than the angels.
But now,
all
broken,
wounded,
compromised,
stained.
But God ...

At the dreariest hour,
God broke through
the darkness of
our winter with
the great and eternal light
of His Son.

Christmas Is About the World

"hy, it is she that has got all Narnia under her thumb. It's she that makes it always winter. Always winter and never Christmas; think of that!" [1]

—*The Lion, the Witch, and the Wardrobe*

I wholeheartedly agree with Lucy's response: "How awful!" I remember how weary I would get when winter in the Chicago area never seemed to end, sometimes running into March or even April. It stayed cold and gray and lifeless so long. Still, I can't imagine living in uninterrupted winter. And no Christmas? Truly dreadful!

Today, we mark time by the birth of Christ. Our calendars are ordered against that pivotal event in history, but for centuries the world truly was locked in a state of perpetual winter. There was no Christmas.

Just as C.S. Lewis's imaginary land of Narnia was frozen under an evil enchantment with no hope of a coming springtime thaw, so our world was plagued by a chilling curse that petrified the hearts of humanity. That long winter produced lives of futility void of light, life, and color … without the expectation of Christmas.

This was the condition of the world into which Christ was born. And such is the state of each human being on our planet who has not received the gift of Christmas.

God never does anything by chance or without intentionality. He never makes mistakes. It was not a random event; it was, in fact, quite on purpose that God determined the exact season, the exact moment, and the exact location for the introduction of His Son to our cold, bleak world. Christmas came during the winter solstice, the darkest days of the year. At the dreariest hour God broke through the darkness of our winter with the great and eternal light of His Son. God invites us in our darkest days to embrace light and warmth and hope, to leave winter behind, and to welcome Christmas into our world.

Christmas is about the world, because God's love never ends and it is enough for us all.

For God so loved the world.

For God so loved the

that He gave...

Christmas

is about

world,

Giving.

For God so

loved the world, that

He gave ...

Christmas
is about Giving.
God gave,
when Christmas came,
the perfect Gift,
the
indescribable gift,
the heavenly gift of God's grace
that will not fade away.
The free gift,
eternal,
always living,
given
once
for All!

Christmas is
about the giving
of a gift that
will not fade
away.

Christmas Is About Giving

y brothers hated wrapping gifts. To them it was a necessary but troublesome part of Christmas. When I volunteered to help out, they gladly delegated all of their gift-wrapping to me. I grabbed the card table from the hall closet and set up a gift-wrapping center in my bedroom. This became an annual tradition; I wrapped all the gifts, including my own. With each individual family member in mind, I added creativity to decorating his or her gift—unique papers, ribbons, paper doilies, and other ornamentation.

And I never peeked at my own gifts; I didn't want to spoil that magical moment on Christmas Day.

I loved giving and receiving gifts, but I discovered, as all children do, that the gifts of Christmas morning fade as playthings break, interests change, and our desires become more sophisticated. Trinkets and toys fail to satisfy what we really long for at Christmas. Like most of us, I found myself hoping for a gift with my name on it that would last. Something that had staying power after all the tinsel and trimmings were boxed up and put away until the next year. I was looking for a gift that would not fade away. It was not to be found under a tree.

Little by little, I was learning that Christmas was not about the exchanging of gifts, but about the giving of Christ … The Gift. His wrappings were not the shiny, decorative trimmings of our holiday celebrations, but the coarse, muslin-like cloth of the common man. He was presented to us in a feeding trough rather than under a festively decorated tree. Yet, He was, and is, the perfect gift.

Christmas is about giving. Compelled by love, God gave the only Christmas gift that will last forever. He is the perfect gift, sufficient for everyone.

For God so
loved the world,
that He gave
His only Son...

loved ... ...d that He gave His only Son ...

Jesus.

For God so
the worl

Christmas

is about

Christmas
is about Jesus.
The Son,
the only Son of God.
The Word
in the beginning.
Creator of all things.
The Lamb,
the image of the invisible God.
In Him all the fullness of deity dwells.
In Him all things hold together.
He is
the same yesterday, today, and forever.
In all things made like us.
The Light
of the world.

Christmas is a celebration
of heaven-sent,
life-altering,
world-changing truths.
The Word,
the perfect Gift,
came to us.

Christmas Is About Jesus

hristmas is not about nostalgia or memories. Christmas is not "for children," nor is it about creating "a spirit of giving" or a "season of cheer." Christmas is a celebration of heaven-sent, life-altering, world-changing truths. God came to us. He became like us, He lived to redeem us, and He died to save us. Christianity alone is the story of how and why God came to earth.

Christmas was the moment of His first appearing, His incarnation.

And what an appearing it was! Though austere and humble, it was at the same time monumental and grand—a supernatural choral announcement by a host of angels appearing in the sky, speaking to men and singing by the thousands; a star that shone exceptionally bright and stood still in one place; kings that traveled for two years to give gifts and to worship. This was no ordinary birth.

Today, beaming new parents send out e-mail blasts to hundreds of family members and friends, but no mass circulation of good news can compare with God's miraculous Christmas proclamation. The birth announcement of the Christ child was sent to the far reaches of the universe.

As a teenager, I remember longing to capture for myself the true meaning wrapped up in this glorious incarnation. I envied friends whose families attended Christmas Eve mass or midnight services. It seemed to me that being in church at the stroke of twelve would somehow bring a greater touch of inspiration to the holiday that I loved. Intuitively, I knew there was much more to understand about the gift of Christ.

The Book of John opens with this statement: "In the beginning was the Word, and the Word was with God, and the Word was God," then declares, "And the Word became flesh and dwelt among us." To appreciate the magnitude of the greatest Gift, we must know the Word and the treasures of its promises. As we know the Word, we can know the Christ, the image of the invisible God who never changes.

Christmas is about Jesus, the perfect Gift, who came to our world out of love to be our Immanuel … God with us.

God so loved the world, that He gave his only Son.

Christmas

is about

For God so loved that
whoever believes
in Him

For God so

loved the world,

that He gave His only Son,

that

whoever believes in Him...

Christmas
is about Choice.
Whoever believes
receives
opens the door,
shall be white as snow
adopted
heir of God
partaker of the Divine Nature
lavished with the riches of grace
made alive together with Him.
Forgiven.
Beloved.
Chosen of God.

A door is
at the same time
both an entrance
and an exit.
Whoever believes
may come in and all
who enter are welcome.

Christmas Is About Choice

In the summer of my sixteenth year, I fell in love. Not with a boy but with architecture. I had the privilege of spending much of that summer studying with a group of American students in the small town of Quimper in western France. Every weekend we traveled by bus to tour castles, chateaus, museums, cathedrals, and countryside towns and villages. A week in Paris was the grand finale. I loved it all.

I learned the difference between Roman and Gothic architecture. I discovered spires, stained-glass windows, entrances, and arches. I gained great appreciation for the artistic mastery in the statues and gargoyles that adorned the cathedrals and chateaus. I learned that much of the artistry was designed to tell the story of the Bible and the history of the church to the many who could not read.

But the doors were my favorite feature, perhaps because I could see them more closely than the spires towering hundreds of feet in the air. There were grand doors, carved doors, Gothic doors, and massive entrances covered with beautifully crafted symbols. Even the more ordinary doors were carved with simple, decorative elements.

Thinking back on that summer and the beautiful architecture I learned to love, I thought again about the doors and realized: a door is at the same time both an entrance and an exit. By passing through it we leave one realm and enter another.

With the gift of His Son at Christmas, God set before each of us a doorway. He invites us to walk through the open door, leaving behind our unbelief and entering the life-giving realm of faith.

My childhood dream of Christmas lasting forever was within reach. The invitation of Christmas is always open.

Christmas is about choice. Whoever believes may come in and all who enter are welcome.

For God so loved the
that He ga
that whoever be
in Him s

Christmas *is about*

For God so loved

the world, that He gave

His only Son,

that whoever believes in Him

should not perish...

Christmas
is about Hope.
That we shall not perish.
Earthquakes
Floods
Storms
Wars
Persecutions
Famines
Death
But we who believe have hope.
All will be made alive!
All things will be made new!
All will see Him face to face!
The anchor
of our souls,
firm and secure.

This is the
hope of Christmas—
Immanuel,
God with us—
even when our hearts
are broken and
we feel we will perish.

Hope.

Christmas Is About Hope

n June of 2008, my sweet precious granddaughter, Molly Ann Mutz, was born full term with congestive heart failure, due to a serious malformation of blood vessels in her brain. Molly, who was beautiful and perfectly normal on the outside, lived only seven days.

What comfort is there for my daughter and her husband who were so quickly separated from their first-born child? Will they have joy again? More to the point: will their heart-wrenching longing to see Molly again ever be quieted?

If Christmas had not come, the answer would be "No." The end of life would be the end of everything.

But Christmas did come! Jesus was born! And He gave the world many promises: new life in Him today, forgiveness for our wrongs today, and the assurance of heaven where all things will be made new forever. "And I heard a loud voice from the throne saying, 'Behold, the dwelling place of God is with man. He will dwell with them, and they will be His people, and God Himself will be with them as their God. He will wipe away every tear from their eyes, and death shall be no more, neither shall there be mourning nor crying nor pain anymore, for the former things have passed away.' And he who was seated on the throne said, 'Behold, I am making all things new'" (Revelation 21:3-5a).

These are words of hope to a young couple who had to plan a funeral instead of a homecoming. They are words of hope for me, for I wanted with all my heart to rescue my daughter and son-in-law from such pain. Though I had no power to rescue them, Jesus does. He alone can redeem our pain and turn great sorrow into joy.

This is the hope of Christmas—Immanuel, God with us—even when our hearts are broken and we feel we will perish in the flood of grief and loss and all that appears meaningless.

In *The Brothers Karamazov*, Fyodor Dostoevsky wrote, "I believe like a child that suffering will be healed and made up for, that all the humiliating absurdity of human contradictions will vanish like a pitiful mirage ... that in the world's finale, at the moment of eternal harmony, something so precious will come to pass that it will suffice for all hearts."[2]

Christmas is about hope. I, too, believe and have hope because Christmas has come.

For God so loved the world, that He gave His only Son, that whoever believes in Him should not perish

Christmas

is about
Eternal

For God so loved the world
that He gave His only
that whoever believes in Him
should not perish but ha

Life.

eternal life.

For God so loved
the world, that He gave
His only Son,
that whoever believes in Him
should not perish,
but have eternal life.

Christmas
is about Eternal Life.
By faith
made alive,
registered in heaven,
given a new name
in the Lamb's Book of Life.
No eye has seen
no ear has heard
no mind conceived
what God has prepared for those
who love Him.
In the heavenly city
whose builder is God
which is to come
on that Day when the Lion of Judah appears
at the sound of the trumpet!

s about
Eternal Life.

Eternal life
 is the glorious destiny
  of all who believe,
a place where all things
   will be made new,
 where Christmas
   will never end.

Christmas Is About Eternal Life

od created us to live forever with Him. It was His intention from before time began. Tragically, life without end was interrupted for all in the garden event. The life God intended for man—without pain, without loneliness, without fear, without loss—was gone in an instant. At that moment, death entered the human experience.

Yet within each of us is a God-inspired longing for perfection that was lost so long ago.

Eternal life means death is not final, but merely a doorway to the heavenly city God is building. It will be a place of great beauty and radiance with streets of gold, gates of pearl, and walls adorned with every kind of precious stone. It will be free from all evil and all who enter "will see His face" (Revelation 22:4). "In the face of God, we will see the fulfillment of all the longing we have ever had to know perfect love, peace, and joy, and to know truth and justice, holiness and wisdom, good-ness and power, and glory and beauty."[3] And in that majestic place, there will be no night, and "no need of sun or moon to shine on it, for the glory of God gives it light" (Revelation 21:23).

When He welcomes us home at the sound of the trumpet all will be made right, "all things [will be made] new" (Revelation 21:5) and "no longer will there be anything accursed" (Revelation 22:3). All who believe will be made whole in body, soul, and spirit.

My son will not stumble because of his neuromuscular disease. He will have strong legs and strong muscles and he will run. He will run like the wind.

My friend will not be shackled by lifelong diabetes. She will enjoy food with delight.

My nephew will not be held back by autism. He will welcome family and friends without fear.

My loved one and friend will not be driven by emotional disorders. He will be unencumbered.

My sweet baby granddaughter will not be separated from us any longer. She will dance with us all one day.

And the triumphant joy of all things made new will have just begun. We will be with Jesus forever and without interruption again. And we will know that "in Your presence there is fullness of joy; at Your right hand are pleasures forevermore" (Psalm 16:11).

Christmas is about eternal life. This is the destiny of all who believe in the gift of Jesus. All because Christmas came.

For God so loved the world, that He gave His only Son, that whoever believes in Him should not perish but have eternal life.

Christmas is about promise.

The unchanging nature

of His purpose.

For it is impossible for God to lie.

His Word is true,

sure, sacred, inspired.

His precious and magnificent promises

will never fail.

He is not slow about His promise,

not wishing for any to perish

But for all to come to repentance.

He is near.

The time is near.

All will come to pass

in the twinkling of an eye!

Come quickly, Lord Jesus, Prince of Peace,

Wonderful Counselor,

our Immanuel!

Christmas

is about Promise.

Even though the heart is universally recognized as the symbol of love, a simple red heart cannot begin to represent the depth and breadth of God's love for his children. This heart is an attempt to blend the shape for love with some of the symbols of God's expressions of love throughout history.

The earth is our stage in the theater of time. The universe is the backdrop and the surrounding curtains for the drama of God's amazing redemption story in which He is the playwright, the director, and the audience. Our planet and we who live on it are the continual focus of God's love.

Giving at Christmas began with God. It was His idea and the essence of His great love to give good gifts to His children. We love because He first loved us and we give because He modeled giving. With the ultimate in cost and sacrifice for His first and only Christmas present, God gave once for all.

From the grandeur of the expanding universe to the minuscule first cells of human life, the Creator of immensity reduced Himself to the confines of a tiny invisible fetus. As we humans greet our newborns with an inspection of tiny feet and hands, Jesus too entered our world in the body of a precious newborn. His incarnation is symbolized by the small feet of a baby in a manger.

It is beyond human comprehension to understand how God can be our audience of one and also be directing the play, yet it is somehow true. The door represents our free will as humans. God created us with the ability to reason and to formulate plans and to make choices, millions of choices over a lifetime. And the most important choice is whether we will open the door of faith and believe there is life beyond the here and now and that Jesus Christ is the way to that life in eternity.

In church history the shape of an anchor has been often used to represent the stability and unshakable nature of the Christian faith. There is the suggestion of the cross in its shape, there are many illustrations referencing ships and waves and storms in the Bible, and there are stories of first-century believers martyred by being drowned attached to an anchor. Life is fragile, subject to violent storms and often terribly unpredictable. We need hope to live life without despair. The anchor symbolizes for believers in Christ the hope of the unchangeable promises we desperately need to survive and thrive in life.

One day the curtain will close on the play of life. On that Day, eternity will begin with the sound of a trumpet. This will mark the triumph of the Gift of love, the Door of faith, and the Anchor of our hope. On that Day, Christmas will begin to last forever!

When that trumpet sounds, Jesus will appear and all will see Him. One of His names in the Bible is the Lion of Judah who is the king of God's people. As a lion is commonly known as the king of all animals, so is Jesus the King over all creation. His first appearing when Christmas came was as a tiny babe, but His second appearing will be as King, and then all will know that He alone is King and Lord over all!

END NOTES

1. C. S. Lewis, *The Lion, the Witch, and the Wardrobe* (New York, NY: HarperCollins Publishers, 1950), 19.

2. Fyodor Dostoevsky, *The Brothers Karamazov*, trans. Constance Garnett (New York, NY: Barnes & Noble Books, 2004), 218.

3. Wayne Grudem, *Systematic Theology* (Great Britain: Inter-Varsity Press; Grand Rapids, MI: Zondervan Publishing House, 1994), 1164.

ACKNOWLEDGMENTS

To be believed in is a wonderful gift.

I have received that beautiful present from two new friends, Rebecca Price and Rob Jorgensen. Their enthusiasm for my initial ideas and designs was so encouraging I felt almost giddy. The joy of working with these two has been a gift "that keeps on giving." And for Dennis, my best friend and spouse of thirty-six years, who first believed in me so many years ago, I will always be grateful. I am a changed woman because of his investment of belief in me.

Cheerleaders extraordinaire are our adult kids, especially Ashley and Laura who, along with Dennis, had some very good suggestions that have made this book much better.

And thanks to David Uttley and his team for the design work. What a treat to work with you again.

Of course, every good and perfect gift is from God Himself. His Spirit, reminding me of truths in His Living Word, is the ultimate Creator of every detail of this book. He is my Source and I am grateful every day to belong to Him.

With Christmas love to all of you,
Barbara

Barbara Rainey is a mother to six adult children, five of whom are married and have given her fourteen grandchildren. She and her husband, Dennis, cofounded FamilyLife, an international ministry to families and marriages. They have coauthored a number of best-selling books including *Moments With You* and *Moments Together for Couples.*

As a gifted communicator and watercolor artist, she has also written and illustrated *Thanksgiving: A Time to Remember.* "I love the holidays of faith—Thanksgiving, Christmas, Easter—because they can, if we let them, touch our mundane ordinary lives with the sacred," says Barbara.

As part of her family's Christmas preparations, Barbara looks forward to setting out her old-fashioned red tinsel tree, baking her grandmother's pound cake, and celebrating the stunning Gift of Christmas, Jesus Christ.